2020

Enjoy your
"trip" to Krakow!

♡

Sherilyn   Christmas 2020
A virtual tour.

CONTENTS

PREFACE

Little explanation. I have travelled through many countries on four continents. Travel experiences have always been an important part of my very being, as well as the topic of my doctoral dissertation, researching the deepest, most essential values and qualities of travel phenomenon. Poland is where I was born, and tourism has always been my career. It's a wonderful business and great passion. This book of reflections and stories says it all. Many years. Many travels. Many tours, places, events. And most important: You. Many clients, guests, official visitors to Poland from the governments, politics, show-business, universities, and global companies, as well as business partners. People from all over the world who became my friends, some of them very close, and who, before they came to Poland for the first time, may not have known what to expect, or just expected something else.

This book is not a typical guide-book, the type easily found wherever books are sold. It is the fruit of passion, I believe, and the key to Polish culture, history, and thought. I want you to feel like you are on a walk with me, on the drive, or sitting at a table in the garden facing the biggest mediaeval square in

Europe, full of people, spectacle, and deep charm. Many times, I have been told by my guests, clients, and friends to set down in writing my reflections, dialogues, observations, conclusions that we have often raised during our journeys. Tours that I have designed, guided, and operated, that we carried out hundreds of times throughout Poland and elsewhere, and that have always revealed to us some experiences not-easy to describe, from the *in-between* world.

As for the Doctor of Philosophy and travel studies, as well as long-time private guide and founder of an awarded travel company, the journey or tour means, first of all, our internal and external dialogue evoked while travelling. In a dynamic, irregular, out-of-home state of our minds and a rhythm beyond our routines. In openness and unexpectedness to which travel motivates us so often. It all happens while sightseeing, walking, driving, exploring, and facing the reality with ideals. We may be amazed, surprised or simply pleased just sitting by the table, talking, absorbing, and while meeting the others first of all. The others who may become the prism through which we experience everything we encounter. The process of touring in wider picture and in its core is the relationship between us and what we share during travels. Culture, words, observations, knowledge, history, business, enjoyment, beauty, time, space, dreams, expectations, and future always coming now. We may be shocked sometimes: we may reflect on similarities and differences but also on who we are due to our travels.

On the crossroads of various historical, cultural, political, and mental currents Poland has existed for over 1000 years, with its beautiful but complicated history and story. In the heart of Europe, the moments we experience while travelling, may open us for some new perspectives and ideas of what Poland means. Realms that were hidden for long time and not allowed even to be shared with the world. The last two centuries of dramatic events, and especially the cold-war freeze that, to a large degree, froze our opportunity to travel. Opportunity to meet, to talk, to get to know each other and in the same time to share our heritage, to reflect, and to act together. These are always the highest values of our journey through the world. Let's spend such moments together now, please. Let's spend these moments in form of the short essays, stories, facts, hints, sometimes even poetic reflections and conclusions. Let's be inspired. And let's always remember to smile.

Christopher Skutela Ph.D.

KRAKOW

The sun is setting over the Old Town's square. *Rynek.*
Talking like river flowing between us. Everybody feels together.
Walking through Krakow, sitting in cafés,
thinking of old and new together.
Spirit in the zoom.
Artists, celebrities, travellers, students,
everybody stops for the moment here.
People and places, it has always been fascinating.
Society, culture, political life, start up.
Cheese cake, pope's cake, blueberries, and tea,
water, apple juice and *lody.*
To wander, to dwell, to meet and keep finding.
Routes of different worlds culminate here.
The journey begins somewhere between us.

Krakow, with its charm, intimacy, and spectacle, inspires such moments. All year round. Coffee is good, a special time, but the deepest values of Krakow emanate from its always vibrant culture of people in all its different levels. Beyond a wealth of museums, monuments, historical buildings, and theatres, there are so many festivals and events of every kind. Impossible to follow them all. Churches, synagogues, universities, museums. Narrow streets and hidden squares. Parks. Shopping malls. Food markets and flea markets. Artistic boutiques. Restaurants and luxurious hotels. Treasures and history on every street corner, culture, and modern initiatives in the not-too-big, eminently walkable city. World-known objects patronize over the down-to-street inspirational atmosphere. Criss-crossing is a norm in Krakow.

Krakow might be called the "Heart of Poland." It used to be the capital. It was chosen the European Capital of Culture in the year 2000. In 1978, the Historic Center of Krakow and the Wieliczka and Bochnia Royal Salt Mines were among the first of twelve world sites to appear on the UNESCO Heritage List (Auschwitz-Birkenau was added in 1979). The same year, Karol Wojtyła, Archbishop of Krakow, was elected pope and moved from Krakow to Rome becoming John Paul II. As the pope he visited over 100 countries and the city of Krakow seven times. So many tourists visit it repeatedly as well. You may live in this city for years, but on every visit to *Rynek* and the Old Town, you will believe you are seeing it for the first time. It's a magnetism of *genius loci*. Spirit of Polish history, culture and faith at a glance. Krakow is a zoom for Poland and for Central Europe. What creates this phenomenon is a story to discover by ourselves.

- Wawel Royal Castle, Main Market Square, Royal Route, University Quarter, Kazimierz Jewish District, Former Ghetto in Podgórze and Schindler's Factory are the areas in Krakow with the highest number of visitors from all over the world. 14 million of visits in the city and the region as for 2019. More than 90% of visitors feel satisfied, comfortable, and very safe. Here we are.

- Take a walk along św. Tomasza Street, and you may notice a board by the café *Pożegnanie z Afryką* (Farewell to Africa). It commemorates the Polish diplomat Jerzy Kulczycki. In Vienna he opened one of the first cafés in Europe. Please check his story and you will be amazed.

- Do we often walk together, taking a break in café or park, trying to feel the moment and place, to think, to laugh, to understand, to be? What makes the real encounter different from an online talk?

| Krakow, Main Market Square |

- Throughout Poland, in most of towns and cities, you will notice signboards saying "*Lody.*" Poles love ice cream. In every possible form. Especially, but not only, in the summer. There are places so crowded that you can't take a seat, and the line of waiting customers may be very long. 100 people or more. Poles love to walk, so they stop here and there to enjoy, to taste, to talk, to spend family time and then go further.

WARSAW

Warsaw is in the center of Poland and a little bit to the right when you look at the map. It is commonly thought of as Eastern Europe, but the center of Europe is actually further east. For some, it is considered one of the biggest business hubs of Central Europe, the city of new adventures and ideas to come. For some, it is the city of contrasts where what you see while walking the streets brings you the vision of the Kingdom of Poland, the 1800's, the interwar times, the communist regime, and postmodernity all together. The last two periods are especially visible in Warsaw's architecture.

When you stand at *Plac Grzybowski,* on one hand you see the monumental church of All Saints. On the other, there are pre-war tenements and nearby modern skyscrapers; behind one of them is *Nożyk* Synagogue, the only surviving pre-war Jewish house of prayer in Warsaw. Behind all of these, flying in the air (soaring above), is the "gift of Uncle Joe Stalin" - Palace of Culture and Science - surrounded by other buildings in the architectural style of socialist realism. How could you ask for more? The history of the last centuries surrounds you: a thousand stories to tell, imagination chasing the imperceptible in this not so well-known spot for tourists. Nearby, there are many well-known historical and cultural objects significant to all of us. But the nearest, most palpable, seems to be always the ever-present impression, weight of tragedy that this city endured during World War II. In fact, we are inside the area of what was once the biggest Jewish ghetto in Europe, created here by German Nazis in 1940.

How much this city suffered - we *cannot* imagine. How many people and futures were lost exceeds our ability to comprehend. Warsaw is a symbol of fight, bravery, and determination in the face of cruel adversity; of tragedy. Warsaw had the largest Jewish ghetto in Europe. Warsaw had two uprisings. Few cities have ever suffered the destruction wreaked upon Warsaw. When you see pictures in the museums, when you ride by tram among not-so-pretty hundreds of socialist buildings that replaced the destroyed beauty of the past, when you stand over the empty holes of graves at the Jewish cemetery where some families had hidden for months to avoid extermination, you just want to maintain a respectful silence ... . And then, speak it loudly so everybody can hear and see and try to do something not to make it happen again and again. About 85% of Warsaw was razed to the ground by Hitler's order in 1944. In 1939, the population of our capital was about 1.3 million. In 1945, it was about 420,000. How does this horror speak to us?

- From *Plac Grzybowski,* you may take a walk to not well known former New Jerusalem district. Sounds interesting, doesn't it? The other direction takes you to the area of famous *Mila 18*. This title, from the novel by Leon Uris, brings to the minds of many what happened here.

- In 1987, Pope John Paul II celebrated Mass at All Saints church. Among thousands of the faithful was Mother Theresa of Calcutta. Both were very happy to be able to visit Poland, officially still under communist regime.

- Please visit the Warsaw Uprising Museum and Polin Museum. Both will complementarily build a background of what happened before and during World War II. They will also reveal hundreds of lesser known facts, aspects, subtleties.

| Warsaw, Plac Grzybowski |

- *Canaletto* was invited to Warsaw by the last Polish king. He painted landscapes of our beautiful capital. Would he have ever thought such disaster would befall the city when he painted it? His art was used to rebuild it.

ZAKOPANE

Did you see *Quo Vadis* or *Solaris*? Both are Hollywood movies based on Polish novels, and both writers stayed in Zakopane many times. They were inspired by the mountains and culture of the region. Brilliance accompanied their writing. Henryk Sienkiewicz was awarded the Nobel Prize for *Quo Vadis,* and Stanisław Lem was considered one of best-ever science-fiction writers. Have you heard of Karol Szymanowski? Probably the second most famous Polish composer, after Chopin. Szymanowski lived in Zakopane in a beautiful wooden villa named *Atma* ("spirit" in Sanskrit). Szymanowski's works have been played in the finest concert halls all over the world. This is just a very limited representation of artists who used to walk on narrow Zakopane streets and climb the steep Tatra trails.

There is a place in Zakopane called Pęksowy Brzyzek. It is the oldest wooden church and cemetery in the city. The cemetery is a national monument where many famous Poles are buried. Each grave is sculpture. In wood, granite stones and glass paintings, the life of the person buried is manifested and illustrated. Burial grave as a symbol of biography. Each grave is a piece of art. Writers, climbers, physicians and politicians,

17

sculptors, nuns, skiers and guides, rescuers, painters, and local members of resistance movements from World War II, all together represented on a small plot hidden among trees in the center of Zakopane. Think about this place when you watch the movies. Think about the effort that the art and literature require. Transcendence may be easier in the mountains.

- In cemeteries like this, we commemorate people, their lives, their deeds. We cultivate a whole culture as well. Through meditation over the graves we may build part of our future of culture and humanity. Silence brings values and new ideas.

- Very often while entering the small wooden church by the Pęksowy Brzyzek cemetery, we encounter weddings. Most locals are dressed in colorful, elegant folk costumes which they still use on special occasions. Most aspects of local traditions are still evident, including dress codes, music, and meals in fantastic restaurants. Walking Krupówki Street – the best-known shopping district in Zakopane, full of great restaurant gardens to relax – horse carriages with tourists may be observed. Driven by highlanders dressed in black hats, white shirts, and cream-colored trousers, with decorative motifs typical for this region. *Parzenica* is one of the most remarkable of these motifs. It is heart-shaped and heart-touching pattern used not only in the handicraft. It stays with us, drawing patterns in the memories not to forget this particular part of the world, and not to forget about love which can be found in the mountains.

| Zakopane, near Pęksowy Brzyzek |

AUSCHWITZ

For years, I have visited Auschwitz–Birkenau probably a thousand times. I have been there with the famous from Hollywood, with well-known politicians and representatives of different nations, with owners of global companies, professors, rabbis, artists, priests, with people from various backgrounds. On the drive, we always seem to have the same thoughts running through our heads. Where am I going? Why am I doing this? How could it happen? What will be most difficult for me there? Will we ever be able to stop such atrocities? It's like going under the judgement of my own thoughts, beliefs, attitudes, feelings, imagination. And this process is never finally done. There is simply too much for our hearts and minds. You cannot hear and think and speak of little children killed like this, of all these families and friends, their relations, their plans and lives, their hopes and dreams, their efforts, careers, properties. All this was stopped, finished, plundered, liquidated.

We cannot think of this. We do not want to. We are afraid. In some way perhaps we shouldn't. But in some way, we should. And we must. Everyone dies. We prepare ourselves to pass away; yet, we are not fully ready. The victims of the Holocaust were *extracted* from the world like weeds. Golden seeds of unrepeatable, incomparable personalities treated like they would never have any dignity or value. Like nothing. Like there would be no possibility. Humans worse than animals or even plants. Golden souls with golden thoughts treated like waste, consigned to the abyss. Their gold teeth were extracted from the mouths later. Such was the disaster of millions perpetrated by others who felt right, justified, and proud to do so. As if they were gods. Places like Auschwitz show the extraordinary heights and depths of behavior of which humans are capable. We can be holy. We may even give our lives for somebody we don't know. We can also do the worst: slaughter with no sorrow or regret, with absolute indifference, like reckless robots in an evil absurdity as millions cry.

| Auschwitz-Birkenau. Photography of liberated children. |

- Hannah Arendt's trip to Jerusalem to observe the trial of Adolf Eichmann in 1961 motivated her to coin the phrase "banality of evil," not implying lack of conscious awareness by Nazi actions but lack of reflective rationality when actions lead to an atrocity against others.

- So many camps around occupied Europe, so many millions of people killed. Yet, from time to time, signs of hope. St. Maximilian Kolbe sacrificed his life voluntarily for an other man in Auschwitz, saying his fellow prisoners to have hope always even at the moment of death. Witold Pilecki, Jan Karski, Irena Sendler, Family Ulm, Sophie Scholl. So many heroes, so brave, righteous among the nations, ordinary people with extraordinary selflessness. People who carried the lights of hope through the times of unspeakable darkness.

• Auschwitz-Birkenau as the Memorial and Museum of Former German Nazi Concentration and Extermination Camp is visited each year by over two million of people. It is good news. All the better when more young adults are among them. This site, along with all other places of genocide and atrocity inflicted on people in different moments of history, may be treated as a universal symbol and warning. The importance of such memorials is to encourage us and raise reflection on our human, moral condition, to build a better present for our nations together, and to avoid behaviour in our daily lives that could lead us, step by step, unnoticeably, to tragedy.

DO NOT BE AFRAID

"Do not be afraid," he said, while at the loggia of St. Peter's Basilica in Rome. It was 1978. A century ago, in 1920, Karol Wojtyła was born in the small town of Wadowice. A one-hour drive from Krakow in the foothills of the Beskidy mountains, part of the Carpathians. This was always his playground. The town is fantastic, all renovated after his death, including the building with the apartment where he lived during the first eighteen years of his life. It is just by the main square of the town and next to the pretty church. A whole building became the museum of his life, beliefs, and all that he has done for the world. His journey from this little town to the esteemed place in world history will touch your heart and soul. One of his best friends, Jerzy Kluger, with whom he used to play football as a boy, is commemorated there too. The Jewish community was quite large, as it used to be in many Polish towns before war. They stayed great friends until death of John Paul II in 2005.

At the back of the museum, and in many other places in fact too, we may sit for a moment and contemplate, while eating famous papal cream cakes. Once, while here after Mass, the pope started to reminisce about his younger years. After exams, they were often going to the confectionery nearby, often eating too many cream cakes :) So sweet was his goodness, so deep was his wisdom. His love for every person and his willingness to engage in a dialogue, even when he disagreed, were reflected with power within his life.

It was all reflected as well within lives of many other Polish saints. Their places are now being visited much. Sister Faustina, Jerzy Popiełuszko, Maximilian Kolbe, mentioning just a few of the 1900's, who, in many sites across Poland, left a deep mark of love and mercy. Popiełuszko's grave in Warsaw, Kolbe's cell in Auschwitz, Sister Faustina's tomb in Krakow, ... The Sanctuary of Divine Mercy in Krakow in some way speaks about it all. From here, as John Paul II remarked once, the spark of the divine mercy will come forth to the world and prepare it. Hundreds of thousands of pilgrims come here each year to pray in front of the image of Merciful Jesus.

- Do you know that the Diary by Saint Faustina is one of the most translated of Polish books? Revelations and thoughts for new times seem to be very demanded around the globe. And even more now.

| Wadowice, Museum of St. John Paul II |

- You may find online English-language movies, sometimes by world-renowned directors, showing different perspectives of the lives of Polish saints.

- Polish Catholic folklore is very evident in its different manifestations. Corpus Christi feast with colorful processions throughout streets, or All Saints and All Souls days with millions of lights and flowers on graves, are just some of the most noticeable examples. While driving, we constantly pass by roadside shrines in various styles and sizes, although some of them were removed or destroyed during the wars and communism.

BLACK MADONNA

One of the three most visited places in Poland is situated close to its centre: Bright Mount. The Black Madonna takes care of Polish hearts, as many say and believe. She is the Queen of Poland. The history of the place dates to 1382, and the history of the icon much further in the past. We must go back perhaps to the beginning of Christianity. This Image of Mary with Jesus could have been painted by first Christians, perhaps on the table from the Holy Family's house. What's most important for the Polish nation is that, throughout the last centuries, millions of prayers, meetings and hopes were expressed under this icon by pilgrims and passers-by who just stopped here for the moment. Something special is in the air - as we say in common language - it brings to the heart reminders of Polish faith and *fate*.

Poland has been predominantly Catholic from its beginning. For 1000 years and even longer. Everybody has heard of Black Madonna – Mother of God of Częstochowa. Bright Mount became the symbol of our complicated history, and a phenomenon of a nation searching for its identity in both heaven and earth. This is especially true during so many wars and moments of occupation. This site is one of the main moments to understand the Polishness on its way through history, and on its attempts to believe that we have the mission to live it. Here is a sense, a deeper sense, not only of our personal existence but of the life of whole nation as well.

- Each year, over 100,000 people walk to Częstochowa from different regions of the country. From a few days to a few weeks, mainly in July and August. It is phenomenon of having painful blisters on your feet while rejoicing at the same time - singing together on empty fields, on paths and on the busy streets of cities.

- In 1655, the famous defense of Częstochowa happened. A much smaller group of Poles managed to defend Bright Mount against Swedish invaders. This event became one of the defining moments for Polish identity and sense of community.

- Why is the Queen of Poland called black? The darker representation of Mary and Jesus is most probably caused by mix of paints and distemper, as well as varnish applied a few times throughout the centuries. Who knows how much darker the true Mary and Jesus may have been?

EUROPE

The geographical center of Europe is about 160 km / 100 miles north-east of Warsaw, in Suchowola. Would you ever think of Poland as Western Europe? No. Eastern Europe? Yes. In fact, *we are* Central Europe, that's for sure :) Crossroads of history, culture, religion, economy and ideas are somewhere around. The Cold War pushed us to the Eastern Europe because Central Europe was erased from the maps and the general awareness of the public in the West.

Ladies and gentlemen, the Iron Curtain was really quite iron - and ironic! People could not travel. Products were not in circulation too. Knowledge, information, experiences could not be shared easily during that strange era of being somewhere there to the east. Grey times, not great. Therefore, we are still often considered as being eastern but it is fine. We can even be western :), throwing a little stone of facts into the garden of the world full of information. With the open heart for friendship and smiles. Always :)

Poland's central location may be both a blessing and a curse. Driving south of Poland, I can only see beauty of diversity in Europe. Within a relatively small geographical area, you have a colorful and plentiful range of states, nations, languages, ethnic groups, religious denominations, cultural customs, food, architecture, music. Driving zigzag south from Krakow, every few hours we can enter another country. A dozen of them within a few days? Yes, it is possible, but of course it's better to have a month or more :) The mosaic is so rich and unpredictable. It all shows well our location. Within half a day's travel, you can reach five capitals. The moment we become aware of this enriches us forever. Now you can imagine a cosmos of diversity as well as permanent trials of being wise, reasonable and respectful at the same time. Location.

| Suchowola, Geographical Center of Europe |

- There are a few central points designated for Europe by geographers, and all of them are situated in, or very near to, Poland. There is no reason and sense to make any comparison of countries, but the location always implies a lot and determines geopolitics. No state as we know should develop at the cost of another. This is the inherent obligation wherever we live.

- Is it coincidence that Jerzy Popiełuszko was born in

Suchowola? He was murdered in 1984 under the communist regime as the priest associated with the opposition Solidarity trade union. He used to travel across Poland, and taught the working class that every person has rights and dignity. He was threatened a few times by his murderers, but he loved everybody, including his oppressors. They lived by persecuting others, but he lived to tell simple truths – as he remarked many times. Recognized as a martyr by the Roman Catholic Church, he often quoted St. Paul: "Overcome evil with good." His life was started in the geographical center of Europe.

- The European Union is a wonderful expression of institutionalized coexistence, cooperation and friendship. No control at the borders and openness in many aspects make it desirable by most Poles. In 2004 Poland joined the EU. However, the euro currency is not popular among Poles. This is similar to the situation for example in Denmark, Sweden, Hungary or the Czech Republic. We have our good, old Polish Złoty (PLN), and we like it very much. :) Many economists value it as well. *Złoty* means "golden."

DRIVING

Welcome. We're driving through Poland. The roads are fine. They get better each year. It is a must to improve after the communist oppression, when travelling could not be very important and people were, simply speaking, poor. Now we have cars from different markets, and we have highways towards our future. Poland is under construction again, being built and rebuilt thanks to many who sacrificed their lives, careers, personal freedom. You can stop at the petrol station for good coffee or a meal; everything seems quite clean. On the road, you can turn to the side and see smaller towns with newer sidewalks and streetlights. You can talk to your friend and guide, who is driving you, about all and everything Poland - where we have two Poles, we have three opinions ;)

While driving through landscapes – the fields, woods, mountains, lakes - it is good to enjoy the Polish philosophical nature, so often found in our history. Road trips may open minds and hearts, and Poland is drivable all over with good infrastructure, hotels and everything you need. Horizons are wider, especially when we are off the main roads. Less-travelled trails paint complete pictures. Zamość or Przemyśl, Lublin or

Chełm, Białystok, Suwałki, Olsztyn and Koszalin, Szczecin, Gorzów and Zielona Góra, Jelenia Góra, Opole, Kalisz and Bytom, Gliwice, Bielsko-Biała, Kielce, Tarnów, Rzeszów, and many more names from the road signs will remain in your memory. Tiny towns in between, National Parks and Nature Reserves, hidden gems and forgotten treasures. The list of stops while driving is long. The list of experiences and reflections on travel is infinite. We will try hotdogs at some petrol stations, but not so many as dots on a Polish map :)

- Zamość is a well-known reservoir of Renaissance architecture in Poland. Recognized on the UNESCO World Heritage List, it is, however, on the very east side of the country, therefore, it is not visited as often as it should be. Driving to Zamość itself will make you happy to experience green woods, nature parks, and beautiful fields. In Zamość, like in a "Little Florence," you will feel the bloom of humanity. Vicinity of Ukraine may become invitation to visit our neighbors and magnificent city of Lviv, which for hundreds of years used to be Poland. This might be real act of humanistic adventure, cultural travel, fascinating road trip.

| Driving through Poland |

- Jelenia Góra is another example of a hidden treasures of our country. Small sized city, but it is home to many historical buildings amongst the beautiful Karkonosze mountains. Many health resorts are nearby, as is the Valley of Palaces and Gardens, out of which many are turned into luxurious hotels with marvelous views and magnificent spas. Driving there is like a route of 100 breathtaking stops.

- Train travel through Poland guarantees many memorable experiences too. Good, interesting adventures. Some lines are still oldish, but most of them very well-renovated. The main ones are quite elegant. Breakfast or lunch on the train, Wi-Fi, silence, modern shapes and comfortable seats with tables, and most of all, the remarkable landscapes of Poland. Variety of 100 landscapes and more ... in the rhythm of the train.

GDAŃSK

Gdańsk was for long time known as *Danzig*. Daniel Gabriel Fahrenheit was born here. The Solidarity Party captured world's attention and imagination, and the world changed thanks to it. Some walls fell … These are just a few words of examples that could describe this special city. It was one of the richest in the past, from where the grains and treasures of Poland were shipped to the world. It was an intercultural hub for many nations, and for the ideas.

The beautiful old town, with sea gulls flying over the roofs and towers. St. Mary's Basilica from which you can see the Baltic and the cranes of famous shipyards. With the heart you can see Poland as we used to measure it: from Krakow to Gdańsk, from the Baltic to the Tatras, from the Westerplatte Peninsula to the cross on top of the Giewont mount. And down there, on the little streets of old Gdańsk, we are seeing people buying the amber, tasting *Goldwasser* and listening to the carillons' music, mixed with the sounds of street artists trying to earn something for their vacations. In the city of different freedoms.

The peninsula where World War II started, the ruins of

military buildings there, remind us that we all carry the values which should be defended until the end. Each of us has such duty, each of us experiences such realms of life. Do we all want to follow these remarks of John Paul II, who has witnessed with power that we *are able to* live in peace in spite of different opinions.This is what Polish soldiers have been doing here from the 1st September 1939. "No more war," says a banner by the Westerplatte Monument, where many leaders of the world appealed. We are all responsible for that. We must start again and again to build this process of reconciliation, and we defend what is most important in life. Standing on top of the mound at Westerplatte, we can feel it with the wind from the sea, we can see these perspectives.

| The Gdańsk Agreement in Shipyard, model in European
Solidarity Centre |

- Look at these bricks over the bricks. Gates, walls,
chambers, towers. The largest Gothic castle in the world,
and the modern bullet train rushing nearby across the
bridge. Sunset makes the view even more spectacular. All
is red. Malbork, in northern Poland, makes such
impression that it is hard to imagine greater complex of
castles and more holistic presentation of mediaeval
civilization. It is easy to get to Malbork by very
comfortable, high-speed trains from Gdańsk. One hour,
and you are amazed.

- By modern highway from Gdansk, we can easily get to Torun as well. The Old Town is on the UNESCO list, and we can find another Teutonic castle there, although in well-preserved ruins. Unknown to many visitors, Torun is the birthplace of Mikołaj Kopernik. He is more commonly known as Nicolaus Copernicus, the astronomer who "stopped the Sun and moved the Earth". Torun is famous of its *piernik,* too – gingerbread. With heart-shaped one in your pocket you may climb the Gothic town hall tower – representative for Central Europe – and watch the Wisła river running below the city, carrying Polish history to the world.

- Within next decade, we hope we will be able to take a picturesque and rich journey on a river cruise from Krakow through Warsaw to Gdańsk and the Baltic Sea, with so many other places to be discovered on the way: Sandomierz, Kazimierz Dolny, Puławy, Góra Kalwaria, Płock, Włocławek, Toruń, Bydgoszcz, treasures of nature and culture, people and places. I can't wait.

ŁÓDŹ

Łódź may deserve to be known as the "Polish Hollywood." Not only for its fertile film school, but also for its very similar name: *Łódź* should be pronounced *Woodz*. Just add the "Holly" and here we go: *Hollywoodz*! Of course, Polish cinematography is quite well-known, but not so many of us have ever heard that Warner Brothers was started by Polish emigrants to USA, that Samuel Goldwyn was Polish, that many people of Hollywood's elite have some Polish roots? Walk the Łódź Walk of Fame and stars will shine for long.

Łódź was once a city of three cultures. Nowadays, it is the third largest city in Poland, with the largest Jewish cemetery in Europe. It also had the best weaving industry in the past, go visit *Manufaktura* today, and you will see the heritage of it in totally new way. Once called the "Polish Manchester," it currently has the very interesting Museum of Design. So many faces you can see of this city while riding the tram from south to north. So many new things may happen here. Łódź is waiting.

- We are walking down Piotrkowska street. We

commemorate Arthur Rubinstein, Marek Edelman, and Julian Tuwim. We remember Israel Poznański, Karol Scheibler, and Ludwik Geyer. We glorify the hero Jan Karski and the writer Władysław Reymont, who himself pictured Łódź as nobody else before him or after him in his novel *The Promised Land*. For *The Peasants*, he was awarded the Nobel Prize. We could commemorate many more wonderful people associated with this city because children of it gave so much to the world, and because this street is one of the longest commercial arteries in Europe.

• Movies by Krzysztof Kieślowski, Andrzej Wajda, Agnieszka Holland, Paweł Pawlikowski, Lech Majewski, Krzysztof Zanussi or Jerzy Skolimowski may be the most inspiring. They always reveal some elements of the Polish vision of the world. Watching them all as well as movies by less-known, but very talented, directors, may become important puzzle-pieces in the bigger picture of Polish culture.

| Studio Cinemas are in different Polish cities |

- In my opinion, Łódź could become one of most modern and lucrative cities of film, business and design. It already became prestigious UNESCO city of film. In my mind's eye, I see skyscrapers in the middle of Poland over well-rooted culture, with all its deep meanings. *Łódź* means "boat" in Polish. This boat may become a good ship, carrying dreams to become reality. Let factory of dreams become so also for the poorest inhabitants of Łódź, whose poverty was produced by communism and post-communist temptations of too-quick wealth by some.

POZNAŃ

Gniezno. The name derives from *gniazdo*. It means "nest." The first capital of Poland was established there, in western Poland, near Poznań. Perhaps Poznań was the main headquarters of the first rulers, but probably both places functioned as "co-capitals." There are speculations about two more locations as well. History has many secrets. Many places commemorate our beginnings, as well as the lifestyle of tribes that created the Polish nation. One thousand years of official history of this country shows all the changes that we can imagine. The borders of Poland were being redrawn so often that people started to think: *flexibility*. King Casimir the Great juggled with political treaties, so the ensuing brotherhood with Lithuania made us one of the biggest, most democratic and most inter-cultural countries.

Flexibility seems to be inherent in Polish history, including creativity, and a certain kind of stubbornness, but in a positive way. :) These values, as well as a sense of hospitality are a part of the Polish way of life. If our first capital was known as "the nest", then the country and its history can be considered "the tree" which many times has been tried to be cut down.

Poznań is the know-how city of entrepreneurship and culture. Its international fairs are among the largest in Europe. St. John's Fair and the Malta Festival are other examples; however, money doesn't create identity in its core. Poland began here because different groups tried to live in unity. Most probably, the first two rulers of Poland, Mieszko I and Bolesław Chrobry, are buried in Poznań. It still remains uncertain for archeologists, but Ostrów Tumski (Cathedral Island) offers to travel across those moments, to travel the past - the adventure that never ends.

Nine hundred years later, after World War I, people of this region fought successfully to become Poland again. The superbrand of Poznań may be based on this capital. History, identity and the new independence. Gates to Poland from the west. Place where we can recognize ourselves. The word Poznań derives from *poznawać:* "to meet, to learn, to know."

- Ignacy Jan Paderewski was a great pianist, composer, and the new Polish nation's Prime Minister, a signatory of the Treaty of Versailles. During World War I, he advocated restoration of Polish independence by touring the USA, and meeting with President Wilson. At the end of 1918, he entered Poznań and gave a speech that started the successful Greater Poland Uprising. When World War II started, he became head of the National Council of

Poland in exile in London. In 1941, he gave many concerts in the USA again, and restarted the Polish Relief Fund. He died suddenly in New York in June, 1941.

- The Renaissance town hall of Poznań is one of its symbols, with mechanical goats butting heads every day at noon. Hundreds of people wait for this to happen, raising their heads high up. A much more serious symbol of the city are crosses symbolizing 1956, when the first demonstration of workers against the communist regime in Poland happened here. Over fifty demonstrators were killed and many more were injured "for God, freedom, law, and bread." Many more demonstrations across Poland were carried out later within the next thirty years. There are uncountable fruits of such events and braveness. One of them is that you can read these words.

| Poznań, by the Chopin Park and Poznań "Fara" Church - treasure of baroque |

WROCŁAW

The "Gnomes of Wrocław" are everywhere. At its main square, by a Jesuit church, at the university, in Cathedral Island, in Nadodrze, and by the Centennial Hall. They tell the story and history of the place: people, city, country. You can read these online and follow the map of the gnomes' seeker. You can play a game to look for them here and there. Sitting on lanterns, climbing the walls, watching through windows, hidden round the corners, meeting on benches, walking across the bridges, ... always "painting" the picture of magic historical connections. Wrocław is a city of many water canals, bridges and little islands, therefore the gnomes just follow locals in this hobby to link "different sides".

In Wrocław, you may see the enormous painting: *The Racławice Panorama*. It is 114 meters long (375 feet). While walking inside specially built rotunda, we become part of the story, *part* of the fight for freedom. It's presented in such a way that sometimes it is hard to recognize a borderline between actual painting and scenography, between us and them, between now and then. Tadeusz Kościuszko was the hero of the battle. Yes, the one whose name you may find all over the globe: as a subway station and bridge in New York; as the monument in the United States Military Academy at West Point; in Washington, DC; in Boston, Chicago, Belarus, France, Switzerland; Mount Kościuszko is mainland Australia's highest mountain. These are just examples.

Kościuszko was ero and the true man of freedom. Have you ever heard, that in 1798, the document which is referred to as Kościuszko's Last Will (Thomas Jefferson was named as the will's executor) stipulated that the proceeds of his estate in America be spent on freeing and educating African-American slaves? ... Today, one of the gnomes of Wrocław is sitting on the horse instead of our hero, just by the main entrance to the rotunda building. And it is a proper symbol of its time, when the gnomes (people dressed so during the happening in 1987) were arrested by communist police as the opponents of the previous system. As you see, the Kościuszko spirit remained in the nation and in the concept of gnomes' creators.

| Wroclaw, The Oder River and Cathedral Island |

- For a long time, Wrocław remained German city. Ironically, after World War II, many Poles from eastern lands lost by Poland in the process of the new division of Europe resettled to Wrocław. Nowadays, in western Poland, the population often originates from the east. You can recognize it easily by some names of restaurants, cafés, hotels, and of course while talking to locals. Young Polish adults, who speak quite well English, will be happy to talk to you about their grandparents' stories.

- In one of the corners of Wrocław's main square, just by St. Elizabeth's Basilica, you can see a modern monument commemorating Dietrich Bonhoeffer, a German evangelical pastor. He has been strongly devoted to ecumenism and readiness to help all victims of any oppressive system, whoever we are. From the beginning, he opposed Nazi movements; therefore, he was imprisoned and murdered just before the end of World War II. Perhaps it became one of determinants for this dimension of Polish religiosity which we can name hospitality. Poland has hosted many times different global summits, meetings and conferences, including, probably the largest ever and most regular, ecumenical meetings of youth held by Taizé community.

- Another great person born in Wrocław was Edith Stein, who was Jewish. Her "philosophy of light," phenomenology, essays on women, political views and religious experiences created one of the most unusual biographies. In spite of realistic chances to escape from Germany, she preferred to manifest her German patriotism by staying and opposing Hitler. Finally gassed in Auschwitz-Birkenau, the martyred Edith Stein became a saint of the Roman Catholic Church.

UPPER SILESIA

We are seeing the backyards of the red-brick poorer tenements. There are little storage bins for the black coal. We are seeing chimneys, mine shafts, mounds of industrial waste; you can smell the smog, clouds of pollution instead of the bright sun. Trams packed with workers with the black shades around their eyes … This could have been an impression fifty years ago passing through Upper Silesia, the most industrialized (in the 1800's and then by communists) region of Poland. Luckily, there were also little joys and benefits that even smog could not swallow, but doesn't it sound sad? How much different is the landscape today? The best of the region is more easily visible. The sky is clear and blue is its color, the greenery of the parks, woods, and some very nice buildings, Sun is shining straight on townsfolk' faces, with the sense of humour that has always been here, even in the dirtier times. I would say: it is one of most interesting communities for sociologists to explore.

This, not Warsaw, is the largest metropolitan area in Poland. It has over three million people. The capital of the region is in Katowice, but what counts is many other cities, situated one by one next to one another. If it would ever become one city, it would be amongst the most populated in European Union. It is the region associated with mines and steelworks due to its one of richest deposits of coal on the old continent. Of course, most of the mines were closed during the last few decades for many reasons, but some still work to provide a balanced variety of sources of energy in Poland. However, the agglomeration is very *green,* with plenty of parks and woods and infrastructure for different healthy activities.

What seems to be most important here, is its unique culture. Upper Silesia is known first for its strong dialect. Every Pole knows this special style of language and accent, easily recognizable from far away. *Godej do mie po ludzku* ("speak to me as a human"), you might hear with the echo of a joke in the voice of the elders, while speaking regular Polish :) The hard work ethos, close family relations, and joyful, direct attitude towards others, constitute the tradition and plenitude of customs here. From the underground world of mines to the deep world of culture. This is the mystery of Upper Silesia.

| Katowice, Nikiszowiec |

- Katowice has been recognized as the UNESCO City of Music. Often underground and subversive, with a long tradition of amateur choirs, orchestras and bands of different genres, from classical, Baroque, and jazz to rock, electronic and rap. Let me just mention Wojciech Kilar, Krystian Zimerman, and Jan Kiepura. Artistry seems to be inspired here by the post-industrial landscapes, a miner-searchers mentality, an atmosphere of close relations, and art nouveau influences. This kind of mysticism is evident for example in the works of Lech Majewski.

- Nikiszowiec might one day be inscribed on the UNESCO

heritage list as more than a dozen other Polish sites. It's an extraordinary coal miners' settlement full of regular red brick *familoks* - specialized multi-family residences for workers of the heavy industry, built usually near to coal mines, at the turn of 1800-1900's. Nowadays, as many mines were closed, such settlements are often poorer, but some of them are tried to be refurbished into a trendy venues, some way even "exotic." Beautifully tiled stoves in the apartments, red or green painted frames of windows, main doors wide-opened and meetings by accordion or mandolin, the little storage bins for coal and tools, or toilets, that were usually situated outside the building or half a flight of stairs, became symbols of *familoks'* architecture and functionality.

- Work and community have always been important here. Gatherings featuring the tastiest cakes and torts are pretty standard :) Shouldn't we all cultivate to some degree these good values and ways of life, of being together responsible for one another at work but also after-work? Sitting at *Café Byfyj* in Nikiszowiec, we can understand, trying the cakes and specialities, we will surely feel the miners' little heaven.

WORLD WAR II

Poland has been one of the main destinations for Jewish emigrants since the late 1400's. The number of Polish Jews started to grow larger than all the other countries in the world. There were majority-Jewish towns, as well as *shtetls,* where their proportion of the population was close to 100%. There were many different groups within the Jewish community in Poland: people who would rather live their own way, and the ones who engaged to a serious degree within the social and political existence of Poland, and in everything that we could define as "Polishness." Relations also varied, from close and very friendly contacts to the degree that some part of our population nowadays have Jewish ancestors, to such that we might be ashamed of living under the same changing clouds. Tragic moments, fortunately, seem to have never been predominant, but tragedies of antisemitism are not forgotten.

World War II changed everything. As always, we are still predominantly Catholic, but we don't have as many Jewish neighbours. The same situation concerns Ukrainians, Germans, Belarusians, and Roma people. Occupation changed Poland's demographics. We lost land, but most of all we lost a larger proportion of our citizens than all other states. In World War II, about 17% of Poles died. Polish Jews suffered the greatest loss, but many Catholics and people of other ethnic, religious, and non-religious communities were also killed. If we check the statistics, we cry. Listening to the stories of particular people and families, we cry even more. Some of us, however, survived and Poland is back. Demographics after communism shifted again. The new millennium has started, but we must remember.

Not so far from Presidential Palace and the Castle,
not so far from Unknown Soldier Grave
and the Cross,
very close to us every day – Ghetto.

Always impression of suffering,
always inside, whoever we are.
Ruins over the ruins,
blood running in its veins and out,
dark canals with so many stories to tell …
That's enough to say!

We cannot translate the suffering,
we just want to speak to live together – Ghetto.

| Westerplatte Peninsula. Ruins from the very beginning of
World War II |

- Ghettos, different types of camps and prisons, round-ups, shootings, tortures, terror, intimidation, persecutions, forced labor, diseases, plunder, poverty, degradation, humiliation, hate, ... so many words crowd our minds, so many feelings flood our hearts. Words are insufficient to describe what really happened and the most difficult situations of choices. Between wrong and the worst. Between evil and bad. So often, only such were the choices of people whose homes were entered and whose children had guns put to their heads.

- So many scenes from the movies you remember. So many poems, memorials and nightmares we may have. So many dreams of Poland being rebuilt. And now, where are we? Every generation must learn a-new, must recover and live with the responsibility for what has happened and what will now happen. Hard to draw something good from such tragedies of war, but we have no choice; we must learn to secure a better future.

- One of the biggest problems Poland faced after 1945 was that we didn't regain true independence. Poland was pushed and just fell from the frying pan into the fire. We couldn't rebuild our sovereignty, our normality. We wouldn't *really* start Poland again until 1989. Let's ask locals across the country and listen to the voice of their experience.

INDEPENDENCE

With different Polish problems, conflicts, mistakes, or wrong decisions in the past and present, we are amazed how we survived. *Jeszcze Polska nie zginęła, kiedy my żyjemy*, the Polish national anthem, seemed to be the soundtrack of our survival. Running with blood for over two hundred years of almost permanent non-existence on maps. We lived underground in the veins of our culture shared from generation to generation, like a Polish wafer during Christmas Eve dinner. Poets, painters, musicians, scientists, mothers and fathers, princes and priests, workers and leaders remembered and fought for the living of Poland and the state being reborn. For the 123 years of the partitions of Poland (1795 - 1918), the hell of the World War II (1939 – 1945), the communist regime, and the absurdity of the Cold War times (1945-1989), probably made us stronger … and we can make a helicopter out of a box of matches. *Polak potrafi* ("Polish can-do" spirit) seems a little ironic, but even more truly describing Polish skills to cope with problems and crises.

We have recently celebrated the 100-year anniversary of regaining Polish independence. We must weigh again and again how to use freedom well. How to be the heart of Europe, with pride and humility simultaneously. How to breathe western and eastern winds with healthy lungs. How to tell the world the story of our enriching experience, so we can all learn from each other and be more attentive.

Poland is an extraordinary *phenomenon*. Sometimes, we cannot even believe that we had kings and queens from the present-day Czech Republic, Hungary, Lithuania, Italy, France, Sweden, Germany. Some of them were freely elected by Polish nobility who in the 1500's developed a unique political system, which gave 10-15% of the population control over Poland's parliament and participation in the royal elections. What other country has developed such a system? Even in our anthem, we refer to a few other countries; as if we would always think internationally. It is true, even if so often it concerns being invaded. In 1791, Poland adopted the world's second, and Europe's first, codified national constitution. It was in force for a very short time because Poland disappeared from the maps, but it lives in us forever and influenced our political system nowadays. Therefore, I like to use the word: "phenomenon." The phenomenon of Polish history, independence, and mentality. The phenomenon of being often behind the scenes. The phenomenon of a future that depends on all of us, on the crossroads of our mutual positions and choices.

| Warsaw, The Tomb of the Unknown Soldier |

- For Poles, the main Independence Day is on November 11th, the day when, in 1918, we officially restored our state after 123 years of non-existence. It was the longest period in our history of being absent from maps, but not being absent in the culture and life of the world. Poland's national poet, Adam Mickiewicz, who never visited Warsaw and Krakow, or Chopin, whose career continued abroad, seem to be best examples of Polish émigré culture in the 1800's. Many geniuses never returned. Many were deported and died, often in far away Siberia. The Polish nation around the world ...

- Arthur Rubinstein, who lived in America from 1939, at the inauguration of the United Nations in 1945, began the concert by stating his deep disappointment that there was no Polish flag and delegation at the conference. He stopped playing the piano and told the audience to stand up, including the Soviets. He played the Polish national anthem, repeating the final part in a great thunderous *forte,* and was rewarded with a great ovation. However, the ovation didn't bring change until 1989.

HERITAGE

My great grandmother, Matilda, died in 2008 after 98 years of life. Her life shows well the changes Poles went through during the last century. She lived through six distinct versions of Poland, and speaking more precisely, of *being* Polish. Sounds strange, doesn't it? She was born in a territory under Prussian Partition. Then, she lived through World War I, after which Poland restored its independence and started to rebuild and reconstitute, but where she lived was a borderland, full of political turmoils and three Silesian Uprisings. In 1939, both Hitler and Stalin divided Poland again, invading it within 17 days from both west and east. In 1945, when this atrocity ended, Poland didn't regain its sovereignty. We fell under Soviet regime for the next 44 years, until 1989. As an old woman, Matilda had seen the Internet and mobile phones, but it was not of her interest anymore. She had experienced too much. Poland became, simply speaking, a state of permanent survival, when often sacrifice was the only way to return again and again.

Many visitors travel to Poland to retrace their past. Ancestry and family heritage are very important reasons to come, very often for the 3rd- or 4th-generation Poles from the USA,

Canada, UK, Israel, Australia, and from the other countries where life threw them. Finding roots often ends with tears. Tears of stories and memories, tears for family members who already passed away. Tears of joy, happiness, and relief, because we are the ones who filled the gap. The ones, who came on a family mission, who, with courage and some effort, found and understood where the family comes from, where my roots are, where the values and culture start. It often creates fruitful relations of friendship with those who are here, with Poles who stayed and who enjoy being reunited after so many generations. It often goes with good dinners, cakes, and toast: for life, health, for family! Many times, I was blessed to experience this with first-time visitors who are now my good friends. Helping with such family reunions always touches the heart to the realms not-from-this-world. And in this way, we build bridges through us and in-between.

- One of Matilda's brothers – Peter – performed in The Singer Midgets troupe. It is still a family mystery if he took part in the iconic 1939 film *The Wizard of Oz*. We know he travelled to the USA with this group around that time. After the war, he returned to Europe. For my children, however, he will always remain the uncle - a character from the musical fantasy :)

| Traditional Houses in the Polish Provinces |

- My wife's great grandmother almost boarded the Titanic! However, in Massachusetts, she lost her husband and second son. She got back to Poland around 1920's and her second son became a partisan hunted by Nazis during World War II.

- Most of the largest emigrations from Poland occurred

during the decades at the turn of the 1800's and 1900's, mainly from the south-east parts of the country. At that time, travel across the ocean was the expedition of a lifetime. People usually sold what they had to fund the travel and maybe have a little something for the beginning of a new life, a dream, somewhere better, there … . Travel was obviously very long and tiring.

- From time to time, we stop in towns and villages. We take pictures of names on road signs. We stop by town halls and traditional houses. We visit churches, cemeteries, synagogues. We knock on doors and almost always these doors open. Most people try to be very helpful. Local priests are often specialists :) in going through records, or in guiding special guests through the church. We see baptismal fonts … . This is the story of adventure to find the roots. This is the power of the Polish identity perhaps, and culture, which does not disappear, even on the other side of the globe, even throughout 100 years or more. It blossoms suddenly between here and there, between locals and visitors. After so many years of war and communism, when people were waiting but the borders were closed, we may finally now visit each other. And ancestors are our guides. This is the blessing!

PEOPLE

Who are we? Citizens of the world. Copernicus, Chopin, Madame Curie, Rubinstein. Were they Polish? Who else? How many Poles are needed to screw in a light bulb? Maybe everybody? All of us! :) This is my philosophical version of one of the jokes we may know. In Poland, however, very few people have ever heard of these "ironies" about Poles from behind-the-ocean. Let me be ironic too, just a tiny bit: I'm waiting for the moment when John Paul II would be known as an American, great of course. Could it be? :) For sure, and for many, he could be an Everyman. He was open to dialogue with every person. Deep patriotism and awareness that category of nation is crucial in history and civilization, coexisted in a wise and peaceful way, within his personal integrity, with the skills of international, global regard and of empathy. He was the man for the whole world, citizen by heart of every country.

There were so many periods of time when we didn't exist on maps, and our culture, science, and development were suppressed, that in some sense, being a citizen of the world (and "underground" world) seems to be a Polish specialty. There were so many Poles who emigrated to spread the wings of talent and career, that sometimes they are not associated with Poland and Polishness. Difficult Polish language and pronunciation played a role here too. Maybe, this is one reason why the idea of Esperanto, the language of hope to communicate all, came from Poland. Esperanto was replaced by English, so I can invite you now in a common language to meet and get to know the Poles – here and there :)

- Do You know how many writers from Poland were awarded the Nobel Prize? Was Lech Wałęsa the only Pole to be awarded the Nobel Peace Prize? Who got two Nobels in two scientific disciplines, and why one of the chemical elements was named Polonium? How many Poles would get the Nobel, and many other awards in different fields of activities?

- Paraffin lamp, windshield wiper, bulletproof vest, movie projector. These are only few of the Polish inventions or of which Poles played a partial but crucial role.

- Let's make a quiz about famous Poles who are not widely considered Polish. My turn: Who was born in Krakow and became one of richest women in history? She used to say: "There are no ugly women, only … ."

| Krakow, Window of Memory in the Schindler's Factory |

72

CZEŚĆ

Cześć. The Polish language sounds like the leaves in the wind. You don't have to know all of these exceptions, declensions and grammatical cases, but when you hear it as a foreigner, you may think it's something very difficult to learn. Indeed, Slavic languages are considered to be among the most complicated in the world. Most young Poles nowadays, however, can speak English. Russian was taught before the 1990's. Many Poles prefer to forget it. After 44 years of associating this language with lost sovereignty, it is understandable. I myself was taught Russian for two years. When I travelled throughout Russia by trans-Siberian railway, it helped, and I value this, as well as some parts of Russian culture and history (and of many other countries too). For people who lived most of their lives under forced communism, Russian is not so pleasant. And not by choice!

Cześć means "Hi." *Szczęść Boże* means "God bless you." Both forms are still in use, although the second one is rather only in churches and mines and represents very well the sounds of the Polish language. *Łódź* – the name of the third largest city in Poland (as you remember;) is another example. Almost only Polish letters in one single word! Should we mention tongue twisters? :) The most difficult however, are cases. In English, we say: beautiful car or cars. In Polish, depending on the context of the sentence: piękny samochód, piękne samochody, pięknymi samochodami, pięknym samochodzie, pięknych samochodach, and so on, and so on. The range of irregularities in written and spoken Polish is very large ... OK, let's mention one of the tongue twisters: W Szczebrzeszynie chrząszcz brzmi w trzcinie. Music to the ears, isn't it :) And poetry in blood.

- Polish is a West Slavic language of the Lechitic group. It began to emerge around the 900's, when Poland was born. The Latin writing system is one of the features of Central European culture. Eastern European countries use Cyrillic. Together with Catholicism, geographical location as well as political and economic history, the language constitutes the above-mentioned categorization. Cold War decision-makers simplified Europe into two parts only. This state of affairs and definitions lasted 44 years. Much too long, but, compared to over 1000 years of Polish history and the age of the language, we can put the matter clear.

- There are schools of Polish for foreigners across the country, where some people start their Polish adventure. Sometimes, the motivation is family heritage, sometimes business, sometimes interests and a desire to have the key to Polish culture. There is always a good reason to join a community of fifty million Polish-speaking people around the globe.

- *Day, ut ia pobrusa, a ti poziwai.* Most Poles cannot understand such language either. This is the first Polish sentence found in historical documents from 1270. How wonderful it would be to put it on the modern t-shirt, cap or mug? How many of us wake up and would be able to say it lovingly while making morning coffee :)? However, in the Kingdom of Poland, it was used rather to describe process of making bread. This historical sentence means: "Let me grind and you will rest." So nice, isn't it? :)

FOLKLORE

How would you pronounce Chochołów in English? Almost in Slovakia but still in Poland, this tiny mountain village has a few dozen traditional wooden houses. It's a typical style from the past, and cottages are still inhabited by locals. Owners can furnish the houses as they wish, but exteriors must stay untouched. Most of them were built during the 1800's. Twice a year, the wooden logs are washed, often with just regular soap and water. Traditional folk costumes and art, local singing dialect and customs, food and mood - travelling in time. Art of imagination is very strong here, and present within Polish folklore and local cultures in many regions. Highlanders, Kurpie, Kashubia, Kuyavia, Upper Silesia, Lublin or Łowicz area, Greater Poland, Lesser Poland, Lemkos. The beautiful adventure to get to know them all and to visit them hidden one by one. The reservoirs incorporated to nowadays world and life offering power of simplicity and continuity to our culture.

In Bieszczady, Sudety, or Gorce, everything seems to be falling from the sky. Inspirations like treasures are being discovered while hiking in mountains, and while relating to the local culture, music, architecture and style. The most beautiful wooden churches and houses hide one from next, and you always enter another little world. Native art and naïve art combine with the depth of local philosophical approach to everything. This is good. And often very funny. There will be rain or there will be no rain :) - according to wisdom of highlanders predicting the weather. Tourists should come no matter.

The sharp, fresh air from the highest parts will not let you be indifferent. And the skyline of rocky Tatra peaks or of other Polish mountains will surprise you every day and every hour. Beauty and spirit of what you experience in Polish folk communities may stay with you forever. It is like meeting the friend who will think about you from now on. It can be in lowlands, lakelands or in post-industrial landscapes of Katowice region (where you may feel like walking on the moon among parks and working people), but touring the local communities and meandering through Polish folklore and regionalism is "being" on a very friendly planet full of artistic visions, simplicity and poetry.

| Shepherds on the Way |

- Amber and paper cuts art, weaving and embroidery, works of wood and glass, Easter eggs and Christmas ornaments, cuisine, music, dances, clothes and legends. You can buy, hear, make, and participate. You can experience and support locals. Every year in the world, thousands of examples of regional folklore disappear from the common consciousness of societies and economy.

- Nikifor Krynicki's statue with the dog interests many passers-by on one of the best-known promenades of Polish health resorts. We are in Krynica-Zdrój. He lived in loneliness and poverty, but after his death he lives in movies, documentaries, and first of all in his naïve art. Small paintings and drawings left by him inspire us and the world, transporting us back to our childhood, seeing life in its simple phenomena. He is the pride of the charming town of Krynica-Zdrój. Jan Kiepura is another symbol here. The tenor, whose voice was admired on the finest stages in Vienna, Paris, Milan, London, New York, and Buenos Aires. You can enjoy the Festival of Jan Kiepura in August, stay longer, drink mineral water, visit the museum of Nikifor, walk the mountains, and then take part in the Economic Forum. From art to the money :) Investment in culture lives longer than our accounts. Beyond the financial profits.

UNKNOWN

Every year in Leżajsk, there are thousands of visitors to *Ohel* of Elimelech. He was one of the first *tzadiks* (righteous, charismatic leaders) in Judaism, and one of the most renowned representatives of Hasidism. *Ohel* means "tent", and it's a little building covering graves of some prominent Jewish rabbis or leaders. From all over the world, pilgrims come to pray over the grave of Elimelech, bringing their problems from Israel, USA, Belgium, Romania, Japan or Russia. In the middle of the night, Hasidic groups may knock on the doors of Polish houses where the keys to the Jewish cemeteries are kept and taken care of.

Eastern Poland, apart from the many Jews who once lived there, was also the home to many Orthodox Christians as well as many Greek-Catholics more to the south-east. They all have built beautiful *tserkvas* with colorful polychromy, graceful towers with signatures, and with enchanting songs sung by the elders of local choirs. Village kind of mysticism present in sacred art.

Japanese tourists' visiting Poland usually include examples of wooden architecture in their itinerary. Therefore, many of the small communities, with their tiny churches being renovated, started to welcome buses and cars with visitors from very far away. Synagogues (although not wooden anymore), *tserkvas* and even an exceptional wooden mosque in Kruszyniany seem to be back on stage of interest in the 21st century. Small towns, empty cemeteries, memories and future - signs of reflections. Numerous manifestations of wisdom can be found in such remote places carrying important stories. Might this be a little miracle of Elimelech?

- There are over 100 Hasidic groups in the world with a few hundred thousand members. Large communities are located for example in Jerusalem, New York, London, Antwerp, Toronto. Most of them originate from Poland. Famous *tzadiks* like Chaim Halberstam from Nowy Sącz or Yaakov Horowitz from Lublin are still remembered vividly in the teachings and stories they left. Most of Hasids were murdered in the Holocaust.

- The green, old wooden mosque in Kruszyniany is a kind of curiosity. Poland never had many Muslims. This particular community originated in the 1300's when Tatars settled here. They later fought side by side with Polish kings to defend the country.

| Staszów, Jewish Cemetery |

- In south-western Poland, you can find two wooden
  Baroque Protestant churches. Both are on the UNESCO
  heritage list and include many beautiful contradictions.
  Protestant churches were rarely wooden and very rarely
  Baroque. Churches of Peace in Jawor and Świdnica as
  they are called, due to the peace made between Catholics
  and Protestants. In fact, in Poland, we did not have much
  of the war and bloody conflict which used to prevail in
  Western Europe.

BREAD

Pierogi means "dumplings." You probably know it - but we have many words for various kinds of dumplings: *buchty, pyzy, kluski, kopytka.* The whole philosophy from the kitchen :) They differ with proportions used and the way to make them, and of course this is just the beginning of Polish cuisine. *Bigos, gołąbki, rosół, żurek, barszcz, sernik, makowiec, … .* I am already hungry :) Tasty is our trip and every region in Poland adds at least a few special dishes to the list of Polish cuisine. Restaurants are outdoing themselves in being the most attractive nowadays. Fusions, innovations, creativity, but we always remember what our mothers and grandmothers used to cook. And they still do. Organic food is just the daily routine for them, and more and more young people get back to home-made meals with huge enthusiasm. Yummy!

And now, the bread. Polish *chleb* attracts many, like the Lord's Prayer ("Our Father") :), and seems to be one of the best in the world. If You visit 100 countries, you may have such an impression. When you enter a bakery in Poland, you may be overwhelmed by the types of bread we have. One hundred is the proper number to count on many occasions. Poland has often been a world potentate in grains, and in agriculture generally. Reviewing statistics, you may easily notice that in almost twenty categories, Poland is in the top ten in global production of crops. Mixed grains, rye, oats, triticale, apples, sugar beets, potatoes, cabbage, raspberries, blueberries, strawberries, currants, sour cherries, mushrooms, this is not all. While driving through Poland, almost every month brings new road-side sellers of freshly picked fruits. It is like changing the menu for all of us. Time to travel à la carte.

- Polish creativity again :) By the tables of Polish homes we have coined very special phrases describing our international fantasies: "Japanese herring" or "fish (usually carp) a'la Greek" are interesting examples. You will not find them in Japan and Greece :) While comparing "Vienna-style eggs" and "Turkish coffee" with what we have in Poland, it is *quite* different :) This is Polish creativity again. We like it, but it was forced in some way by the conditions of life when Poland was closed by its occupying oppressors.

| Polish Table, Highlanders' Feast in Zakopane |

- Global is the story of the Salt Mines near Krakow. Wieliczka and Bochnia, as the complex on the UNESCO list, bring to our minds and lips, one of most lucrative products of Poland in the past - salt! The mines still operate to some degree, but the corridors and chambers are much more a tourist attraction for the world. Saline chandeliers, sculptures, murals, underground lakes, chapels, concert rooms and therapeutic minerals in the air down there, so you can even take retreat to breath deeper. Who would have thought seven hundred years ago that over a million tourists will visit this amazing underground world nowadays?

- Bolesławiec is a well-known Polish pottery exported mostly to the USA and Asia. Long tradition, quality of clay, hard-working manufacturers and pretty designs made it popular all over the world. I have once travelled there with one of the assistants to Ronald Reagan. We have purchased many kilograms of tableware sets and this is a quite common situation. Under communism, *the wives* of American soldiers used to come here by special buses from Germany, buying cups, plates, and bowls. This is the elegance of Poland on the tables of the world :)

- Apart from agriculture, Poland mines, produces, and manufactures a lot. Silver and copper, furniture, windows, doors, shoes and clothes, cosmetics, and yachts, outsourcing and tourism. Export volume is higher every year.

NATURE

The forests are growing. The birds are flying. Nature being taken care of by us, hopefully always. I have heard many times that Poland is really clean, and the beauty of nature exceeded visitors' expectations. We struggle with smog in some cities and areas, but it is getting better the further we recede from our occupied past. We plant trees and drink clear water. We have it in the tap, and we have mineral water bottles on very long shelves. In supermarkets, you can't even decide which one to choose. We have health resorts specialized in all kinds of treatments, and we have thermal waters and exclusive pools with hot springs. We have 23 national parks in Poland, and around 150 landscape parks. There is the sea and the mountains, the lowly and the high. We have rivers, lakelands, highlands, and lowlands. There is even a desert: *yes*, Błędowska, a very tiny one, where you can feel like a Bedouin for five minutes - in Poland! :) There are bears, wolves, deer, and wild boars, lynxes, foxes, eagles, and falcons, storks, and bison.

Pigeons are common too … but more often on the ground among people. They even seem to be cultural creatures trying to earn something with their skilled flight in the most crowded places. Main market squares are their beloved habitat;

they are accepted there as well as on some roofs. You can sometimes see beautiful white flocks of post pigeons trained by their owners circling in the sky. They have names, they have respect, and they can race even 2000 kilometers. Very expensive sometimes. How *differently* nature and pigeons can be perceived in different cultures.

If you ever travel to Israel, Lebanon, Ethiopia, or maybe Chad around December, and if you ever see white storks there, you can easily talk Polish to them. *Dzień dobry.* Around 20% of the world population of storks is from Poland. Little ones are born here and start to fly. Driving through provinces and towns, you may often see big nests of these elegant birds. After winter, many people help in repairing the platforms to support nests on top of the posts, fences, chimneys, and roofs, so when in springtime *bociek* arrives, it feels welcome home again. Online, you may even observe their flights to Africa and back, as well as how they behave while here during summer. The best show is the youngsters learning to fly. They waver on the edges of nests with a question mark over their beaks: should I stay, or should I go? Isn't it right question for all of us?

| Carpathian Mountains, Hiking Trails |

- Think about a day of skiing, possible almost everywhere in southern Poland. Then, after a great lunch, jump into the exclusive hot thermal pools, with views of the snowy peaks … :)

- The white stork is one of the symbols of Poland, and you can buy souvenirs celebrating them in different forms. Made in Poland? :)

- Be sure to watch National Geographic or other documentaries on Polish bison. European bison constitutes one more example of an animal that Poland has the largest population of in the world. *Żubr*, in Polish. We even have a famous vodka, *Żubrówka* :) For some, it is *a more* interesting word than *Żubr* ;)

- Storks, of course, bring children :) Sometimes, we also jump out from the famous Polish cabbage, associated so much with Italian Queen of Poland, Bona Sforza, who implemented various agricultural reforms in the 1500's. In fact, the birth rate of Poland has been rather static for the few last decades.

BALTIC

The Baltic Sea is rather cold and dark, but the shores are very interesting. On Poland's beaches, we generally look *north*. That is quite unusual, isn't it? Most Polish rivers flow north. Our beaches are long, quite wide, and sandy; in some places, there are small cliffs. The most spectacular are moving sand dunes near Łeba. It is one of our national parks, where views remind us of a desert, or even of another planet, especially in the winter. The wind is cold, nobody in the sea waves, and you think that it was worth coming out of season. Seals are happy, sand steals land, fresh breeze, and the sea spray with iodine enters your lungs.

We can travel by bike or by foot to move further along the shore to visit quaint towns by the sea. You can swim, sail, wind-surf, and fish. You can drive from the hotel to the rental house, from the spa to the camping grounds, from the sunrise to sunset, thinking of all you have experienced in life - it may sound like an advertisement of asking yourself important questions while on vacations by the sea. :) Biking from Hel, a thin peninsula with old fishing villages, to Sopot, a luxury resort with the longest wooden pier of Europe, may be one of the best ideas here. Fantastic. Driving along far west to Wolin Island, enjoying the lighthouses and seeing the horizons from top of them, may be another tour in Poland. And there is still so much more to do, as much as the waves might bring to your soul with sounds of different days. Tides.

Sometimes the sunset stays with me for long,
rise in me at midnight, in the morning
and at 3pm forever.
To the darkness we may be closer but later ...
Through the horizons in us
we discover the light,
not the one that shines only for the moment but always
whenever we do listen
to the waves of togetherness.

| The Baltic Sea Coast, Beaches |

- I have walked long sections of Polish seacoast twice with my wife and friends. With backpacks and mainly by foot in the sand. Good effort for many days and deep breaths of the sea spray every day. We even slept a few times on the beaches to enjoy the waves, the stars and the thoughts for the future. Who we are? What should we do? Philosophical travels that we all need.

- Sopot and Opole (in southern Poland) are well known for decades for the festivals of songs. Nowadays of course, we have many more festivals of music but in the times of the Polish People's Republic, these festivals let people have a break from the harsh daily life and listen to some sounds of freedom ... . Interesting fact is that the Sopot Festival was inspired by Władysław Szpilman, a Jewish survivor of the Warsaw Ghetto. Did you see *The Pianist*?

MASURIA

The Masuria region (Mazury) is best known for its Masurian Lakeland in northeastern Poland. Over 2,000 lakes of different sizes are connected with rivers and canals. A system of waterways linking the rivers to the Baltic Sea attracts many. Boats, yachts, canoes, rafts, ferries, and bikes create colorful mosaics of free time activities. Wind is here and blows where it wants. These lands were part of the State of the Teutonic Order, the Duchy of Prussia, Eastern Prussia and the German Empire. Hitler made the area here, near Kętrzyn, one of his fortified headquarters in occupied Europe - Wolf's Lair. While staring at stars at evening from the boat in the middle of the lakes, we can think about this, but first of all our thoughts and feelings may *dance* in much wider perspectives, in which our political views become deeper. Night sky and the universe. It seems that Hitler preferred to stare at dark bunkers instead of trying the deep enough meditation of stars, souls, and humanity. Nature always helps the culture, I believe, to get proper measures and care of everybody, from the smallest to the biggest, from beginning to the end.

Mazury, Mazur, Mazurek. Music to the ears again, isn't it? It arouses plentiful associations. *Mazurek* is a bird. Tiny and

95

beautiful. Eurasian tree sparrow. About 1.5 million pairs live in Poland. *Mazurek* is a cake. Famous and tasty. Prepared traditionally for Easter in Poland with the *sweet* inscription "Hallelujah." *Mazurek* is the Mazurka as well, a Polish national dance in triple meter, popular at the ballrooms of Europe in the 1800's. Chopin, Szymanowski, Dvořák, Debussy, Ravel, or Offenbach, all of them composed mazurkas. The most important for Poles and Poland is, however, this one: *Mazurek Dąbrowskiego* - the National Anthem of Poland. As you know, we can sing it to the skies and the wind blows, put your sails on, the Polish eagle flies :) This could really happen in Masuria; it happens often in sport arenas of the world; and for sure it happened many times in history of our fight. Poles love to sing and dance when it is needed. From the serious songs of independence to the lighter melodies of sailors and youth.

| Masuria, Lake Śniardwy |

- A journey through Masuria may take long days. So many lakes and forests, some marshes and fields of stones, and winding, picturesque roads bordered by old trees. From the largest lake in Poland, Śniardwy, to the deepest one, Lake Hańcza, situated almost in the Kaliningrad region belonging to Russia. From Wigry National Park to the city of Olsztyn on the European Route of Brick Gothic. In the summer, you may rent a yacht and sail along the trail of the Great Masurian Lakes, enjoying nature and music festivals. Even country music in the American style may be heard here (especially in Mrągowo). From the wild, wild West :)

- Poles are good in sailing, but our sportsmen proudly sing the anthem with the eagle on the breast (eagle is the national emblem of Poland) while succeeding in many other sport disciplines too: athletics, football, volleyball, ski jumping, and cycling, just to mention a few among most popular sports. You can check the statistics of Polish successes and you will notice that we are almost unbeatable, for example, in throwing the hammer :) We are also skillful in gliding, climbing, duplicate bridge, timbersports, free diving, dog-sled racing, ice yachting. Poles love such less-known sports, and Mazury could be easily treated as the best land for such activities. There was once the saying that the Polish pilot may fly even on the doors of the barn :) Isn't it amazing?

TATRAS

The "Sleeping Giant," called *Giewont,* is partly covered with clouds. It's like a thick, white featherbed when you dream of the best times. You feel warm and safe, but the peaks are monumental and serious, sharp, and risky. You can feel at one with nature and with yourself in the beauty of these mountains. We are at the southern part of Poland, by the border with Slovakia. The Tatras have so many charming places that even after hiking here for numerous times, you may always feel surprised. The most beautiful views of valleys and peaks, mountain lakes, streams, and spots of all-year-round snow, flora and fauna, and mountain hostels where evenings are spent by talking, by the fireplace.

Polish climbers are grown from these trails and routes. Did you know that, out of all fourteen peaks over 8,000 meters high, in winter, twelve were reached so far, and ten of them firstly by Poles? Winter climbing in the Himalayas is the most challenging. The Tatras always played a great role in this challenge. Furthermore, I have this impression and experience courtesy of *my own feet* (hiking and climbing) that the Tatras radiate mystery and mysticism. For many, it is a deep, spiritual adventure and search. Culture and nature cross one another here in a very inspirational way. When we delve into the depths of these trails' experiences, it seems to come with the breath of effort and overwhelming beauty from out of our civilization. Tatras may teach us the new.

Walking through the stones of nowhere
Dreaming everything be clear here
Beauty, every step inside you
Seeing, streaming from the depths of soul.

Mountain seem like home for feelings,
for the mind and soul be pure.
Sharper thoughts seem to ache but truely
vision of yourself appears. Finding.

| The Tatras, Sleigh Rides with Highlanders |

- Jerzy Kukuczka, Krzysztof Wielicki, Wanda Rutkiewicz, and Andrzej Zawada are world-famous Polish climbers who carved their names in the history of himalaism. Exploration of the most difficult places, as well as extreme expeditions in nature, are, to some degree, a Polish speciality. You can add Marek Kamiński, Aleksander Doba, Władysław Wagner, and Krzysztof Baranowski to the list. Many inspiring books to read.

- A wonderful way to wander through the Tatras is staying in chalets or huts. Most of them are like little simple hostels. Some of them are located near the beautiful, clear waters of mountain lakes. Unforgettable evenings await you.

- In other Polish mountain ranges, you will not experience such high peaks, but surely you may meet fewer people on the trails. If you look for solitude in nature, Bieszczady, Beskid Niski, or Wyspowy may be the perfect idea.

SKYSCRAPERS

In Poland, only Warsaw has modern skyscrapers; a few other high buildings are scattered here and there in the centres of other big cities. Low-rise architecture of varied styles will greet your eyes, with 1000 years of our history, including socialist realism. As hundreds of Central European cities were destroyed to at least some degree during World War II, as well as the later need to accommodate people during the process of industrialization by communists, thousands of simple square and rectangular buildings were erected. Grey blocks of small flats for the grey lives of little people. You better be as *quiet* as a mouse because the regime will crush you with the big iron hammer.

Still, millions of citizens across this part of the old continent live in the socialist blocks – nowadays often private apartments – having to cope with daily life, of course. In Warsaw, as already discussed, an infamous symbol of the communist propaganda, the Palace of Culture and Science, often plays the role of a landmark. This was the plan. Hard to believe, but it is still one of the tallest buildings in Europe. It was built in the 1950's, when the implemented architectural style was not yet the cheapest; now, illuminated at evenings, and we may ride up by lift to see the panorama of the capital. As we travel from city to city, we can see the plentiful colors on the socialist residential structures; balconies may be painted nowadays. Before, you were not allowed to show your individual preference. The government chose the color of a big-part of your life. Now, newer colors, doors, windows, lifts; dreams and search for what it means to be happy.

- During communist times you had to apply to get flat for your family in the block. Usually, you got one room less than you needed. If parents had two children, you got just one room for the children and one for yourselves, which had to be used, of course, as a saloon as well. Saloon sounds ironic here, doesn't it? Small kitchen, small bathroom, little you … . As decades passed, the situation improved slowly. *Really* slowly. Nowadays, it accelerates, and more individual homes are being built; of course some people prefer expensive modern apartments and trendy lofts. However, the best way to experience Polish society is from the level of various streets and roads. You can see the move.

| Warsaw, Palace of Culture and Science |

- At present, the highest building in European Union is being constructed in Warsaw. Just next to it, there is a rescued fragment of the original Ghetto wall. From the top of such buildings, you can also see woods and forests like Kampinos National Park, where many Polish resistors fought and were killed during World War II. If this building had existed at that time, we would have seen to the other side of the River Wisła, where many Soviet soldiers ignored the Warsaw Uprising, refusing to help the Poles "kick out" the German Nazis ruining the city. After the war, as an effect of this ignorance, they could "give" us the high Palace of Culture and Science, and say: look, we can build new, wonderful Poland together (built by the hands of Polish workers on the ruins of the city), almost to the skies ... Here the circle closes. *Propaganda*. By the way, the tallest buildings in Europe are located in Russia.

WAWEL

Wait and you will see. The dragon breathes fire. The statue is big, but the Royal Castle is bigger. Wawel is one of the largest royal residences in Europe. Wawel is the school of history, architecture and art; this is apparent as you merely walk through its courtyards and the cathedral. Wawel is its own "universe" - impossible to imagine or grasp. Most Polish kings, their families, many statesmen, writers, and heroes are buried here. Wawel boasts plenty of exhibitions of different kinds. You can spend at least one day on this hill above Krakow's Old Town, and you will understand that Polish history is not to be comprehended; rather, it is to be *felt*. It is a temple of history, and a spiritual centre for many. So magnificent, that I have never met anybody whose breath wasn't taken away by seeing this splendour!

The dragon really breathes fire. We are waiting for joy to see this. We feel safe because the dragon (archosaur) was defeated once by a boy, but who knows how many versions of this legend already exist. At the foot of the Wawel Castle and Wawel's Dragon Wisła River continues to flow. Kings used these waters much during the golden age of Poland, half millennium ago. Nowadays, we can bike along to the 1000 years old Benedictines

Abbey in Tyniec, or to the Jewish Quarter and where Nazi Ghetto used to be, nearby the Schindler's Factory, and to the Nowa Huta former communist district with hundreds of blocks of flats, which used to look like the city from spy movies.

You can sometimes hear the bells. There are many churches in Krakow, but only on the most special occasions (the election of pope or death of the president), the Royal Sigismund Bell chimes. It will remain long in your heart – deep sound from Wawel Hill. The famous bugle call from St. Mary's Church may be heard, in contrast, each and every hour. The trumpeters climb up the stairs to play it in four directions of the earth. It may be one of the world's oldest traditions. Each day at noon, Polskie Radio broadcasts this melody ... and suddenly it stops, to commemorate the year 1241, when Krakow was invaded by the Tartars. After that, while the city was being rebuilt, it gradually became one of the richest and most cultured capitals of Europe. Wawel always shines above us, with its towers, history, and spiritual power.

| Krakow, The Royal Wawel Castle |

- All three Polish National Bards are buried in the crypts of Wawel; the names of all three - Mickiewicz, Słowacki, and Krasiński – appear on avenues around the centre of Krakow, where You can find universities, libraries, museums, cinemas, and radio-station headquarters. You can find statues and streets honouring Adam Mickiewicz all over the country and elsewhere too. The epic poem of Poland, *Pan Tadeusz*, was his main opus; its invocation is taught to every Polish in school.

- The Royal Wawel Castle owns one of the largest

collections of tapestries in Europe. They are called Jagiellonian tapestries. When World War II broke out, 137 fabrics were luckily transported through Romania, France, and England to Canada, finally to be returned after fifteen years of negotiation!

- Schindler's Factory Museum, as it is often called, is so well-known nowadays, that it may be difficult to imagine the poor conditions and greyness of the district where it is located, just thirty years ago. After the Spielberg movie, ranked by many as top ten in the history of Hollywood productions (Krakow is very often classified among the ten most beautiful cities in Europe), the area and topic got off the ground with this new, international focus. The Jewish Culture Festival in Krakow, one of the biggest and oldest of this type in the world, was already a fixture of Krakow's cultural life. We can enjoy and learn all things Jewish. We can participate in different tours including the ones to movie locations. The Oskar Schindler's apartment is located just below the Wawel Castle and Cathedral. When I visited his grave in Jerusalem's Catholic cemetery, I had the puzzle of all these locations in my mind, the faces of people whom he rescued; they are presented by the main gate to Schindler's Factory nowadays. I had the great honour to meet members of different families who were rescued during the war.

DA VINCI

Leonardo da Vinci's *Lady with an Ermine* seems to be looking elsewhere when you look at the painting of her. She saw a lot, I guess, throughout the last centuries. She saw Hans Frank as well, the German Nazi General Governor who took the confiscated painting from place to place, keeping it very close. Finally, *Lady with an Ermine* was found in his country home in Bavaria. It was returned to Krakow in 1946 to be placed again in the Czartoryski Museum. It is one of only four portraits of women painted by Leonardo, and one of most expensive paintings in the world. Nowadays, still an underpromoted treasure of Poland, the Lady symbolizes the secrets of the city, a visual representation of Krakow's psychological renaissance. Sounds interesting, doesn't it? Krakow was almost untouched during World War II compared to the other large cities of Poland, and Renaissance has always been one of its predominant strengths.

However, World War II deprived us of such a large amount of paintings and objects of art that the cost calculation hits multi-digit numbers. Most of the art was never returned. Treasures were buried or hidden, admired by only a few in secret chambers. Some of them were burnt. Paintings contain untold stories forever, and many of them you can interpret while in Poland. *The Last Judgment* by Memling, *Landscape with the Good Samaritan* by Rembrandt, *Beach in Pourville* by Monet, *Saint Francis in Ecstasy* by El Greco, *Battle of Grunwald* by Jan Matejko. The list of examples is long, the list of the stories behind each of them is much longer. You can *imagine*. Exploring Polish museums, we are filled with beauty, the history of world art, and the history of human desire for it, sometimes turning into a brutal greed, ending with cruelty and injustice.

Some of them burnt and changed into clouds,

imagine colors

that filled your heart.

Breath in, breath out, and you will feel.

Art, stories of time.

Each of us watching and seeing unseen.

Dreaming of one, most occupying,

the most beautiful picture of life, which is true.

We are always part of it.

- *Portrait of a Young Man* by Raphael from the Czartoryski collection is regarded by many historians as the most important painting missing since World War II. It is supposed that the painting would be worth at present about $100 million.

- Maps of hidden art and many other secrets died with Nazis including Hans Frank, who was executed in 1946. What was he thinking when the war was at its end? Was he ever able to contemplate the masterpieces he stole?

- Poland lost over 500,000 individual pieces of art worth over $15 billion during World War II. Further cultural losses included 22 million books, many museums, theatres, cinemas, ...

- Take a selfie with a copy of the *Lady with an Ermine* and try repainting everything at home as your own art. Pictures from Poland may be very creative! By art, we often discover what's lost.

FUTURE

Every fifth person you face on the streets of Krakow is a student. It is one of Europe's academic centres, with one of the oldest universities on the continent. Many students meet at evenings, go to coffee shops and pubs, but they also participate in different cultural initiatives. They are one of the pillars on which Poland, with its unusual ambience, is being constantly rebuilt. These young students may be one of the motors driving the good spirit forward. We find old streets with intimate museums, studio cinemas, unexpected restaurants, and bars. We are surprised by churches and restored synagogues with many people inside, including the young, vibrantly living and planning-proposing what's next. All the educational, cultural, and religious initiatives happen together here, in a variety of configurations. It's hard to distinguish particular trends within this one special super-flow. It often sounds like an orchestra, a new type of band with its still-indefinite show for future.

When is the future? Where is it? What is the role of Poland (and this part of the world) in the global process? In all larger Polish cities, academic life, culture, and technology, as well as spiritual movements, set the rhythm of being open to what is new, while not losing sight of what's traditional and wise. Such a balanced process of renewal, honoring the past and future at once, promotes longevity and helps in surviving the worst. This is a part of the Polish *dream*, to be modern and prosperous *without* retreating from its difficult but essential values. It works in most of cases without any contradiction. It is *not only* a dream, but a fact of life in various places and communities across the earth. We all have daily lives; we all struggle with some difficult problems; the value of encountering the old and new together keep us always alive: thinking, sharing, creating, and sometimes just being, but enjoying the togetherness in these individualistic times. Isn't that what the world is for, life, our relations, travel? This is the culture! This is the joyful journey to take care of. The journey to the future, which is already underway. Now - I believe - and in all of us.

| Krakow, Culture by the River |

- Polish universities and schools offer many programmes in English; therefore, you may meet many foreign students on the streets. Whenever I talk to these students, they express their enjoyment of Poland's dynamic, multi-faceted culture. Some of them remain in Poland to make their living and, perhaps, for their entire life.

- The future always sounds interesting, with new hopes always on the horizon. That's good, however, the future sometimes seems very pretentious - *bombastic* :) Do we all rush to develop, to earn more money? Good, better, best

- where is that *state of mind*? Does it really matter? Does it really happen? Isn't the rush killing the time - killing us sometimes and our possibility to enjoy later the peaceful way? Is it too late? Questions raising questions, but after difficult centuries, Poland faces this risk now. Polish creativity and hard-work skills are important, core values, but moving in an aggressive and speedy way may result in social problems. We know, it is already happening to some degree, but the bigger risk surrounds us in the thicker walls of individualism. The future of Poland and the world is in the balance - it's a narrow path, like walking the tightrope – but we are good travellers through this life of crucial moments, we can succeed :)

Made in the USA
Monee, IL
14 December 2020

52899845R00071